Animal Body Coverings

Why Do
Snakes and Other Animals Have
Scales?

Clare Lewis

heinemann
raintree

To contact Capstone Global Library please call 800-747-4992, or visit our web site www.capstonepub.com

Edited by Clare Lewis and Kristen Mohn
Designed by Richard Parker
Picture research by Svetlana Zhurkin
Production by Victoria Fitzgerald
Originated by Capstone Global Library

Library of Congress Cataloging-in-Publication Data
Lewis, Clare, 1976- author.
 Why do snakes and other animals have scales? / Clare Lewis.
 pages cm.—(Animal body coverings)
 Includes bibliographical references and index.
 ISBN 978-1-4846-2535-4 (hb)—ISBN 978-1-4846-2540-8 (pb)—ISBN 978-1-4846-2550-7 (ebook) 1. Snakes—Juvenile literature. 2. Scales (Reptiles)—Juvenile literature. 3. Body covering (Anatomy)—Juvenile literature. I. Title.
 QL666.O6L64 2016
 597.147—dc23   2015000293

This book has been officially leveled by using the F&P Text Level Gradient™ Leveling System

Acknowledgments
The author and publisher are grateful to the following for permission to reproduce copyright material: Corbis: Clouds Hill Imaging, 12 (inset); Dreamstime: Girishhc, 5 (top left), Howard Chew, 19, Jeff Moore, 5 (right), Peter Leahy, 7; Getty Images: Cosmos Blank, 20, 23; iStockphoto: photographer3431, 11; Shutterstock: Asmus, 16, Audrey Snider-Bell, cover (bottom), 17, 23, bochimsang12, 5 (bottom left), Ew Chee Guan, 23 (pest), Joe Belanger, 12 (back), Matt Jeppson, 4, 8, 22 (bottom), Matteo photos, 14, mycteria (fish scales), cover and throughout, Naypong, back cover (left), 10, 23, Oleg Shipov, 6, 22 (top right), 23, Pete Niesen, 18, 23, reptiles4all, 13, 21, Rich Carey, cover (top), SJ Allen, 15, Vlad61, back cover (right), 9, 22 (top left)

We would like to thank Michael Bright for his invaluable help in the preparation of this book.

Contents

Some words are shown in bold, **like this**. You can find them in the picture glossary on page 23.

Which Animals Have Scales?

Most reptiles have hard, dry scales. Reptiles are **cold-blooded** animals. They lay eggs.

A snake is a type of reptile.

4

Fish have scales, too. Many birds have scales on their ankles and feet.

Very few mammals have scales. Pangolins are mammals with scales.

pangolin

What Are Scales?

Scales are a type of body covering.

Snake and other reptile scales are made from the same **material** as your fingernails and hair.

Fish scales grow out of the skin of the fish.

Some fish scales are small and smooth.
Others are large and spiky.

Are Scales Colorful?

Reptile scales can be very colorful.

The bright colors of this coral snake warn other animals that its bite can hurt them.

Many fish are very colorful.

But the color and patterns on fish do not come from their scales. They come from the skin underneath. Most fish scales have no color.

How Do Scales Protect Animals?

Crocodiles have hard, bony scales on their backs. Their scales are like a suit of armor.

Snakes have thin skin. Their tough scales help to protect them from bites, bumps, and scratches.

Some fish scales are smooth and covered with slippery slime. This helps fish escape from **predators**.

Can Scales Help Animals Catch Their Prey?

Shark scales are like tiny sharp teeth. They make shark skin feel very rough.

The scales move slightly when the shark swims. This helps the shark swim fast after its **prey**.

Wart snakes live in the water. They have
rough, pointy scales. They help the snake
to hold on to fish that it catches.

How Do Scales Help Animals Move?

Snakes have large scales on their bellies. This helps them to glide along the ground.

Many fish scales are small. They often make overlapping layers.

The layers make it easy for fish to bend and move quickly from side to side.

Do Some Snakes Have Special Scales?

Snakes have no eyelids. They cannot blink or close their eyes.

They have clear scales that cover their eyes. The scales protect the eyes from dirt and damage.

Rattlesnakes have special scales on their tails.

The scales rattle together and make a loud noise. This warns **predators** to keep away.

How Do Fish Take Care of Their Scales?

Some **pests** like to live on fish scales. They can hurt the fish.

Salmon try to knock pests off. They scrape their scales against the bottom of the riverbed.

Cleaner fish eat the dead skin and
pests on bigger fish. This helps to keep
the scales on the bigger fish clean.

How Do Snake Scales Grow?

As snakes grow, they get too big for their scaly skin. A layer of skin and scales comes off all at once.

This is called **molting**. Underneath, a new layer of scales is ready.

When snakes molt, they get rid of any ticks or mites that were on their scales.

The new scales are clean and healthy.

Scales Quiz

Which of these pictures shows snake scales?

A

B

C

Picture Glossary

cold-blooded animal that cannot store its own heat in its body. Snakes and other reptiles are cold-blooded.

material substance from which something is made

molt to shed a layer of skin or other body covering

pest tiny animal that lives on and harms a bigger animal

predator animal that hunts and eats other animals

prey animal that is hunted and eaten by predators

Find Out More

Web sites

Facthound offers a safe, fun way to find Internet sites related to this book. All of the sites on Facthound have been researched by our staff.

Here's all you do:

Visit *www.facthound.com*

Type in this code: 9781484625354

Books

Green, Jen. *Snakes* (Amazing Animal Hunters). Mankato, Minn.: Amicus, 2011.

Royston, Angela. *Reptiles* (Animal Classification). Chicago: Heinemann Library, 2015.

Savage, Stephen. *Focus on Fish* (Animal Watch). New York: Gareth Stevens, 2012.

Index